GO AND DO LIKEWISE!

The Parables and Wisdom of Jesus

Retold and iIllustrated by

JOHN HENDRIX

Abrams Books for Young Readers
New York

Jesus's sandals were always dusty.

Jesus didn't call any one place home.

But he was not alone. Alongside Jesus were his students, the twelve disciples. These men were not rich or powerful; they were ordinary people. There was Peter and Andrew, and James and John, the fishermen. There was Philip, Thomas, Thaddeus, Bartholomew, James, Simon and Judas. One of the disciples, Matthew, had even been a tax collector. Jesus had called each one to follow him from the very beginning of his journey.

Jesus and his disciples walked from town to town among the people of Galilee and Judea in Israel, because he was on a mission. He was God's son, sent to be a teacher, a storyteller, a miracle maker, a savior.

But no one, not even his disciples, knew where Jesus was headed. When he spoke to the crowds, he invited all to listen. Jesus's teachings were full of vibrant images—often radically different than what the people had heard before from their Jewish leaders. When he showed up in a town, everyone wondered what Jesus would say that day.

Jesus was quite unusual. He spoke with the authority of a wise and important rabbi. But Jesus spent most of his life in the streets and not in the temple. He touched lepers, and they were healed! He blessed the broken-hearted and had dinner with outcasts. The existing temple authorities and teachers of the law didn't see Jesus as a proper rabbi. At first, they were eager to discredit his teachings and expose him as a fraud. But, as Jesus performed miracles of healing right in front of their eyes and even forgave sins, eventually their annoyance turned into hatred and fear. Who would listen to them if the people followed Jesus?

But Jesus was going somewhere. His journey to find those most in need of him began anew each morning. Jesus walked . . .

. . . and ever since, people have followed him.

JESUS RESTED UPON

a shady rock. As the crowd of townsfolk grew quiet, a skeptical rabbi, an expert in Jewish law, questioned Jesus.

"Teacher, what should I do to live an eternal life with God?"

Jesus turned the question back on the rabbi: "What do the scriptures tell you?"

"Teacher, the law tells us to love the Lord with all of our being, and to love our neighbor as naturally as we love ourselves."

Jesus said, "Yes. Obey this, and you will live forever with God."

Hoping to demonstrate his mastery of the law, the rabbi said, "But can you tell us who, exactly, is our neighbor?"

Jesus told a story.

"Once there was a man, and he was on the dangerous journey from Jerusalem to Jericho. You know how narrow and perilous this way is to travelers."

"It was growing dark, and on a remote stretch of the rocky path, the man was attacked! Thieves who prey on isolated travelers fell upon him. They beat him, stole all his possessions, even took the clothes off his back—and they left him alone to die."

But a priest of God, the ones you see in the temple, was also traveling this lonely road. As he looked upon the dying man, the priest feared for his own life—or perhaps didn't want to get his fine clothes dirty—and passed by him on the other side of the road without stopping to help.

A short time later, a Levite, a person who also worked in the temple, came along the road. He, too, saw the wounded man, and blaming the man for his own carelessness, left him in a puddle of dirt and blood.

A Samaritan soon after came along that dusty road.

One of the very same Samaritans that you see as cursed—the same Samaritans that you despise—saw the injured man, a known enemy, and took pity on him. With a gentle hand, this Samaritan washed and bound the man's wounds. He lifted the man onto his donkey, guided him to a nearby inn, and cared for him the rest of the night. In the morning, the Samaritan took two precious coins and gave them to the innkeeper. "Care for this man, and give him anything he needs. And when I return, I promise to pay for whatever else he owes."

Jesus paused.

He looked at the crowd and then at the doubting rabbi.

"Now, I ask you, who was a neighbor to the man who was a victim?"

The teacher of the law reluctantly replied, "The . . . Samaritan, the one who showed mercy."

Jesus said,

"GO & DO LIKEWISE!"

7

Jesus ascended to a high place, and the crowd followed.
He spoke, teaching all who could hear.

BLESSED...
are those who feel like an empty jar.
God will fill that emptiness
with abundance.

BLESSED...
are those full of mercy, for they,
too, will be shown grace.

BLESSED...
are those who cry, for the Lord sees every tear.
Each one, He will wipe away.

BLESSED...

are those who work for peace.
They understand what it means
to be God's child.

9

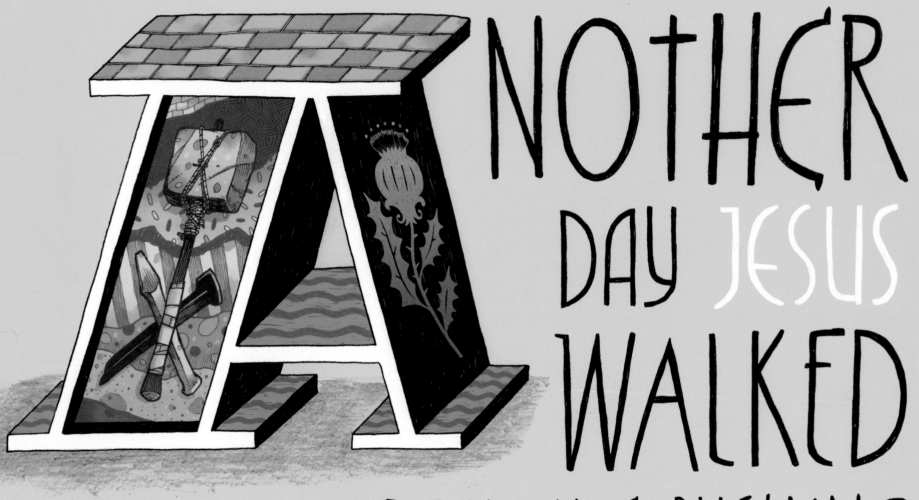

Another DAY JESUS WALKED SLOWLY THROUGH A BUSTLING CROWD.

He stopped and spoke:

"There are many listening to me now. There are some who will hear what I say and obey, building their life upon my words. But there are some who will merely call me 'Lord' but live recklessly. Do you know what that is like? I will show you."

"There was a man, a wise and careful builder, who wanted to build a mighty house. He dug down deep, slowly and carefully. There he laid the foundation stones on the sturdy bedrock."

There was another man, also eager to make a great house. He built well, but did not dig deep, choosing to rest his house upon the sandy banks near the sea.

Soon, the rains came, and the winds blew cold. The oceans and rivers rose, and the roaring waters surrounded both houses.

The tower built upon the firm bedrock stood tall, while the one built upon the sands crumbled and was swallowed by the sea. Everyone who hears but does not obey is like the foolish builder, who trusted the shifting sand instead of the steadfast stone.

The people looked around in amazement, for they had never heard something so clear and sure. This man taught differently than the chief priests, who often relied on other's teachings when they preached.

But Jesus spoke as one with a true authority!

Again Jesus spoke, teaching all who could hear.

"DO NOT

JUDGE CARELESSLY
YOUR BROTHERS AND SISTERS,
BECAUSE YOU, TOO, ARE JUST AS GUILTY.

You come to your brother and say, 'Let me remove this sawdust caught in your eye,'

but all the while there is a mighty branch in your own eye!

How could you possibly see clearly enough

to care for your brother if you

don't first correct

your own

sight?"

Your heart will
naturally tell you to

love your
friends

and despise
your enemies.

But I will show
you a new way:

LOVE THOSE
WHO HATE YOU.

Pray for the ones who hurt you.
Do good to the people who curse you.

It is too easy to love
only the loveable!

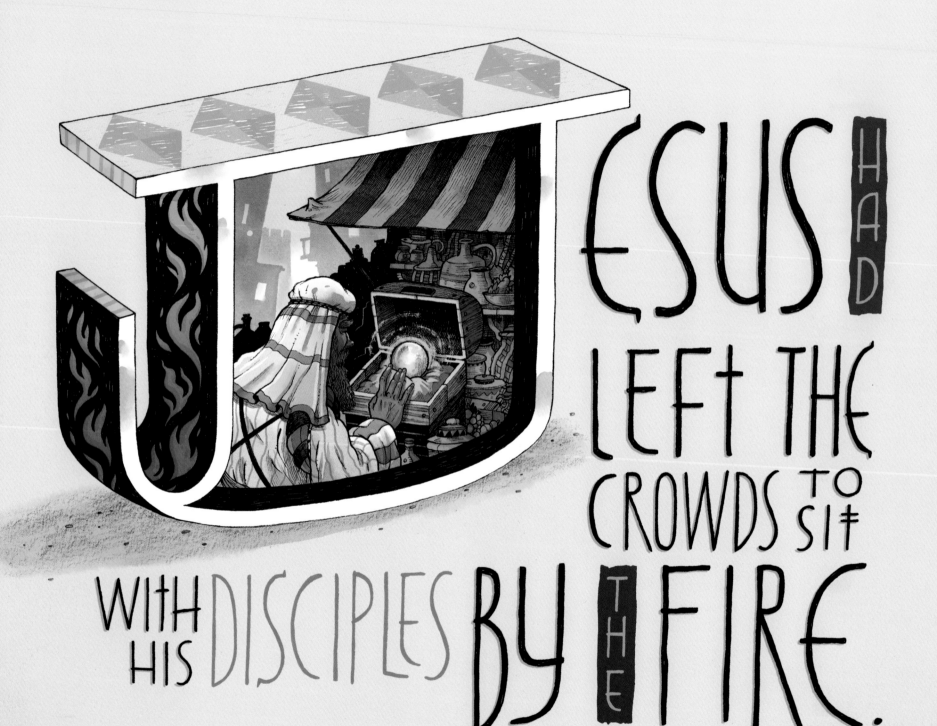

JESUS HAD LEFT THE CROWDS TO SIT WITH HIS DISCIPLES BY THE FIRE.

"BROTHERS, GOD'S KINGDOM,

it will be extraordinary! Imagine a merchant walking through a bustling market. In a dark corner of the bazaar, he sees the most gorgeous pearl imaginable. He wishes to possess it. But he doesn't have enough to afford the great price."

"Still overjoyed, he rushes home and sells every scrap of what he owns in this world—every single thing of value to his name—in order to buy that single pearl."

"God's coming and already present Kingdom will be so priceless, so beautiful, so limitless, there will be no cost too high for those who have truly seen it."

THE · GREAT · PEARL

Jesus spoke, teaching all who could hear.

"Can a hilltop fortress ever be hidden?
Should a lamp be tucked under a veil? No!
You will not be invisible light."

"Through me, you are now God's people.
A people who will be known by light."

"Indeed, you are my high city— I want you to

SHINE!"

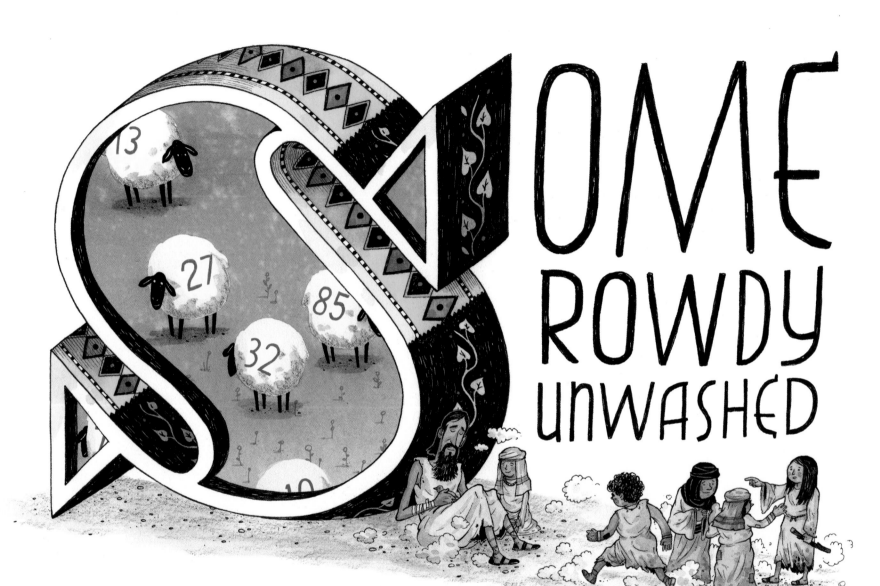

SOME ROWDY UNWASHED CHILDREN

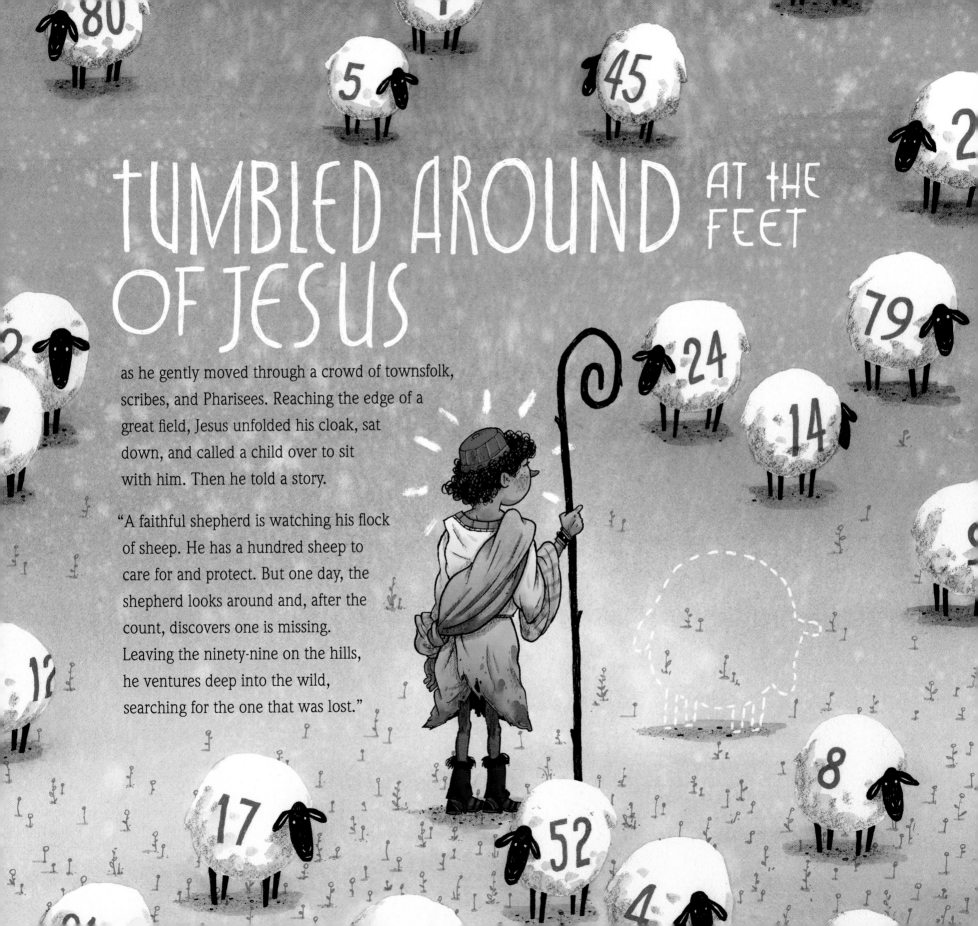

TUMBLED AROUND OF JESUS AT THE FEET

as he gently moved through a crowd of townsfolk, scribes, and Pharisees. Reaching the edge of a great field, Jesus unfolded his cloak, sat down, and called a child over to sit with him. Then he told a story.

"A faithful shepherd is watching his flock of sheep. He has a hundred sheep to care for and protect. But one day, the shepherd looks around and, after the count, discovers one is missing. Leaving the ninety-nine on the hills, he ventures deep into the wild, searching for the one that was lost."

"He searches for hours and finally finds the sheep, stuck fast in a briar bush. The shepherd is filled with joy. Freeing the lost sheep and throwing her over his shoulders, he rushes back home, rejoicing all the way! In fact, he calls his family and friends together, crying out, 'My lost sheep—I have found her! Celebrate with me!'"

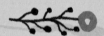

The tax collectors, the teachers of the law, the disciples, and the people looked around at one another.

Lifting a child on his shoulders, Jesus said, "I tell you, there will be more rejoicing in heaven over a single lost soul that has been found than over the ninety-nine in no need of rescue."

"And so it is the will of the Father that none of his children should ever be lost."

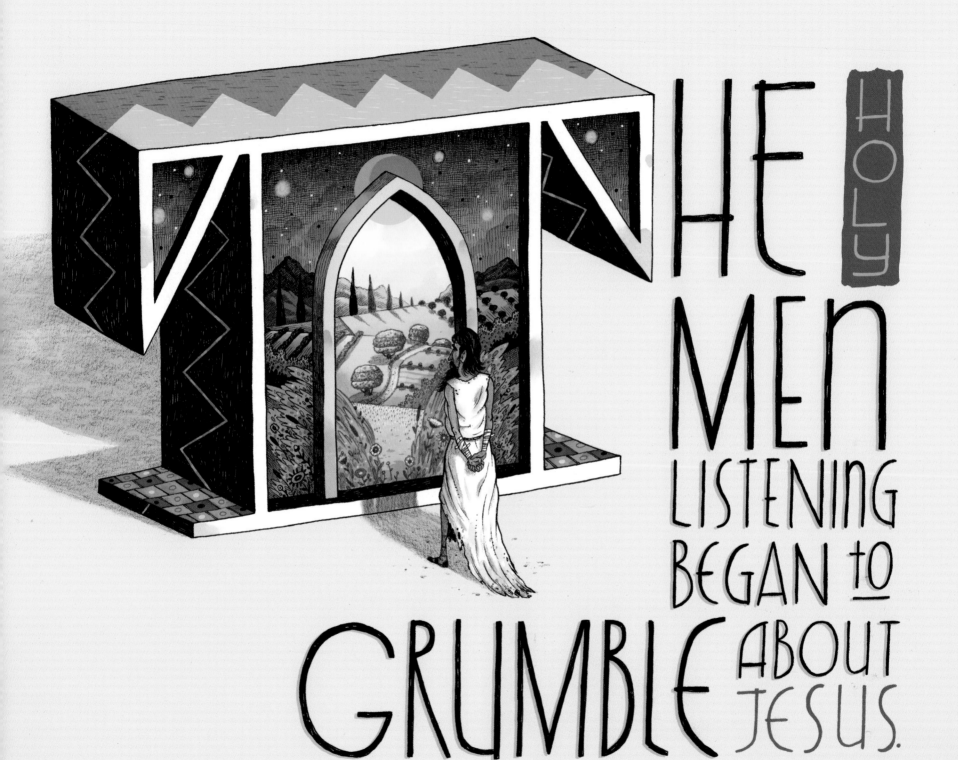

THE HOLY MEN LISTENING BEGAN TO GRUMBLE ABOUT JESUS.

24

They hated how he spoke with the sinners and broke bread with the tax collectors. Now he was telling the sinners that God loved them!

Jesus heard their muttering and told this story.

Once there was a good father who had two sons, and he loved each of them equally. One day, the younger son came to his father and demanded his inheritance.

Although it was insulting to be asked for such a thing, the father nevertheless gave his son his share of the estate. With riches in hand, the son left home and set off for adventure in an exotic land.

25

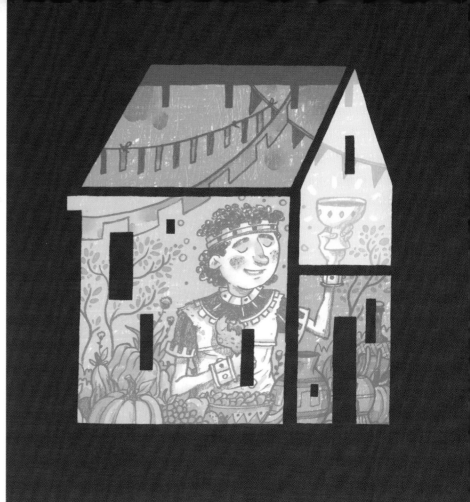

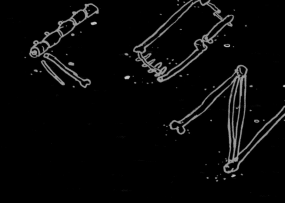

In a far-off country, the younger son squandered his father's wealth, pleasing only himself as he saw fit. Just as the son had spent the last of his fortune, a great famine came to the whole land. He was penniless, hungry, and alone— wandering the streets looking for work. The son managed to get a lowly job feeding pigs. Each day, as the wayward son shoveled out the feed, he ached to fill his empty belly with the dirty husks and pods the muddy swine were eating.

That night, cold and hungry, he gazed back at the eastern horizon toward home. "Even my father's lowly hired men have food to spare every night, and I long to dine with pigs!" the son lamented. In a flash, his folly became clear. "I will go home and return to my father," said the wayward son.

"But I must tell him that I was wrong. I will say, 'I dishonored you, Father. I no longer deserve to be your son . . . treat me like one of your hired men, just so I may dwell in your house again.'"

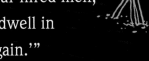

And he began the long journey home, alone with his remorse and sorrow.

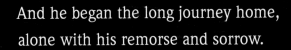

week of travel passed, and the landscape became more familiar. As the wayward son came over the top of a hill he had known since boyhood, he saw his father's house again. As the son prepared for his father's anger, he saw something startling. It was his father, running toward him!

His father's warm embrace was upon him in a rush of joy. He grabbed his son tightly—lifting him off the ground and kissing his cheek!

The son was overcome. He bowed his head and said, "Father, I have sinned against you—I am not worthy to be part of your family—" The father interrupted him and called all his servants.

"Find the best robe, give him new sandals, and dress his hands with rings. Go fetch the very best meat and drink from our cellars and prepare a feast. Tonight, we celebrate my boy who was dead, but now is alive again!"

As the music and dancing began, the smell of the food drifted through the father's estate.

The older son was alone, working hard in the fields, when he saw the commotion taking place at home. Rushing back, he arrived at the party and discovered that his rebellious brother had returned, and that his father was celebrating!

The older son boiled with anger.

He sat alone under an olive tree, refusing to join the party.

His father saw him and came out to speak with him. The older son lashed out. "All these years, I've done my duty, worked hard, and never disobeyed you! I've never had a party like this! That wayward son of yours squanders your wealth, and this is how you reward him?"

Kneeling beside his oldest son, the father said, "My boy, you are always with me, and everything I have has been yours. Today, we rejoice because the dead has come back to life. Your brother was lost, but today, he is found!"

THE SUN DIPPED BELOW

the horizon, and Jesus gathered with his disciples. He sat and shook the dust from his sandals. His journey was coming to an end.

"Where my Father dwells, there are many, many rooms. I am going ahead to prepare a place, just for you, in that great house."

"You can't come with me yet, but you will know how to get there."

His disciple Thomas said, "But Jesus, you can't leave us, we don't know the way!"

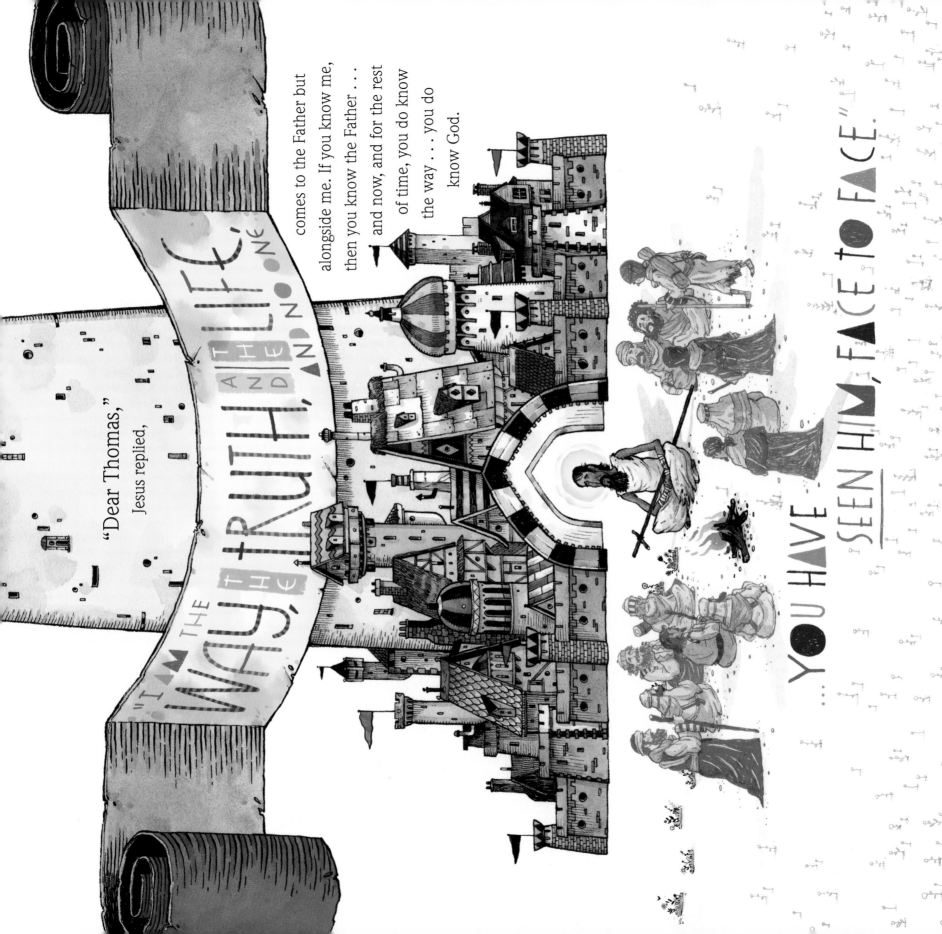

"Dear Thomas," Jesus replied,

"I AM THE WAY, THE TRUTH, AND LIFE.

... No one comes to the Father but alongside me. If you know me, then you know the Father ... and now, and for the rest of time, you do know the way ... you do know God.

... YOU HAVE SEEN HIM, FACE TO FACE."

AUTHOR'S NOTE

For Jesus, the whole wide world was the garment of the living God.
—William Barclay, theologian

Jesus, God's very own son and also God himself, was a miracle walking on earth in the skin of a man. During his life, Jesus taught many different kinds of people—his disciples, Mary Magdalene, Mary and Martha, the chief priests, and the people of Galilee, Samaria, and Judea. Through poignant but simple parables and other vibrant metaphors, Jesus was able to communicate spiritual truths across boundaries of class, race, and education.

The teachings of God are often difficult to understand and visualize. Jesus longed for his audience to contemplate abstract notions such as forgiveness, kinship with God, redemption, calling, hope, wrongdoing, and love. He knew these lofty concepts become more real when anchored in a story. Jesus's parables and teachings were simple, clear, and brilliant. They made difficult ideas concrete and deeply knowable. Through the magic of metaphor, Jesus was able to illuminate more meaning in the story than if he had only given us the mere principles behind them.

In many ways this phenomenon is why I love creating words and images in concert together. It produces a new, unexpected experience. In the mysterious canvas of our hearts and minds, stories, word pictures, and vivid ideas create a deep pool of wonder and understanding. Jesus, with his narrative teaching style, used this new kind of visual theology for us to explore.

Jesus didn't tell parables to simplify or water down God's message to the people—he didn't look down upon his audience. Jesus's stories were a collection of ideas and wise teachings that reached beyond their frameworks. His parables illuminated a complex moral system to an unsophisticated crowd. His stories remind us that God knows our hearts well. Each human was created to be a living story, and so Jesus spoke to us in story—a form that would echo inside our souls for thousands of years. The spark inside our hearts that Jesus the storyteller kindled so long ago still exists today. Human beings need stories that create conviction in us, that challenge our assumptions, and call us to action.

RETELLING VS. TRANSLATING

There are roughly thirty-seven parables of Jesus in the New Testament and many additional pictorial phrases that, though not categorized as parables, are memorable. The act of reasonably abridging the teaching of Jesus is impossible. So this modest collection of his words is presented with great humility. There are many more parables and teachings I wish I could have fit into this brief collection.

To create the text for this book, I have taken Jesus's direct teachings as found in the gospel accounts of the Bible and paraphrased them in my own language. I have sought to preserve the core ideas of Jesus's teachings, but in some cases I have added contemporary phrasing, added incidental dialogue, or added additional context. I did this not to improve Jesus's words, but for audience clarity, artistic purposes, and to bring the reader more deeply into the story. I have been careful not to add any extraneous ideas not found in the Biblical accounts. I'd like to thank Peter C. Watson, MA in exegetical theology, and Pastor Michael Gordon, Master of Divinity, for their advice and expertise in crafting a retelling that honors the Biblical accounts.

This book is neither exegetical nor hermeneutical, but rather a retelling for young audiences. Exegesis asks, "What did the text originally mean?"; hermeneutics asks "What does the text mean today?" I have not sourced the original Greek and Hebrew manuscripts, nor is this a line-for-line retranslation of the direct Gospel accounts. If you would like to read the Bible stories directly, I'd recommend the English Standard Version (ESV) or the New International Version (NIV), the two main translations I used in my study for this retelling. I'd also recommend *The Message: The Bible in Contemporary Language* by Eugene H. Peterson, a wonderful book that rewrites the New Testament in present-day language. That volume was a great help to me as a young Christian and contributed to the inspiration for this book. I believe there is immense value in hearing familiar stories in new ways, and my aim is to help readers imagine themselves as the first audience of these words.

SOURCES

The order of the parables and teachings in this book was created primarily for narrative and thematic flow. The setting of the story is not meant to reflect a single day's events, and the stories are not presented in the chronological order found in Gospel accounts.

Here is a list of the Biblical texts I used for reference, in the order in which they appear in this book:

To the Most-est Rev. Jim Musser,
pastor to young people, minister to all, friend

ABOUT THE ART: The illustrations in this book are meant to be both fantastical and historical. Elements of the images are metaphorical, for artistic purposes (like the setting for the Sermon on the Mount), while visually set in the factual times of Jesus. I took care to research trees (for example, the "Cedars of Lebanon" on page 2), the look of agricultural fields (like figs, wheat, olives), flowers, and fauna from the lands of Galilee and Jerusalem. Clothing (including the priestly garments), buildings, and tools are editorialized but based on visual reference I found in a wonderful collection of books on the culture of first-century Palestine. Some of these titles include *Jesus and His Times* (Reader's Digest Association, 1987); *Illustrated Bible Dictionary* (Barbour Publishing, 2013); *A Visual Guide to Gospel Events* (Baker Books, 2010); and *In the Steps of Jesus* (Zondervan, 2006).

ON THE JACKET: In Matthew 6:25–30, part of the Sermon on the Mount, as Jesus speaks of the beauty of the lilies and birds, he tells his listeners to put worries for tomorrow aside—a reminder of how much God cares for His creation, and how much more God loves us.

The images in this book were drawn with Blackwing 602 pencils and pen and ink on Strathmore 500 Bristol.
The drawings were colored with Golden Fluid acrylics, Liquitex inks, and digital brushes by Kyle T. Webster.

Cataloging-in-Publication Data has been applied for and may be obtained from the Library of Congress.

ISBN 978-1-4197-3705-3

Text and illustrations copyright © 2021 John Hendrix
Edited by Howard W. Reeves
Book design by John Hendrix and Max Temescu

Printed and bound in China
10 9 8 7 6 5 4 3 2

Abrams® is a registered trademark of Harry N. Abrams, Inc.

ABRAMS The Art of Books
195 Broadway, New York, NY 10007
abramsbooks.com